LIFE AFTER DYSTONIA

WITHDRAWN
From the
Mish Penn Harris Public Library

LIBBY KARNS

LIFE AFTER DYSTONIA

YOU CAN HAVE A HOPE AND A FUTURE, TOO!

**Property of
Mishawaka-Penn-Harris
Public Library
Mishawaka, Indiana**

TATE PUBLISHING
AND ENTERPRISES, LLC

Life After Dystonia
Copyright © 2016 by Libby Karns. All rights reserved.

No part of this publication may be reproduced, stored in a retrieval system or transmitted in any way by any means, electronic, mechanical, photocopy, recording or otherwise without the prior permission of the author except as provided by USA copyright law.

Scripture quotations marked (AMP) are taken from the *Amplified Bible*, Copyright © 1954, 1958, 1962, 1964, 1965, 1987 by The Lockman Foundation. Used by permission.

This book is designed to provide accurate and authoritative information with regard to the subject matter covered. This information is given with the understanding that neither the author nor Tate Publishing, LLC is engaged in rendering legal, professional advice. Since the details of your situation are fact dependent, you should additionally seek the services of a competent professional.

The opinions expressed by the author are not necessarily those of Tate Publishing, LLC.

Published by Tate Publishing & Enterprises, LLC
127 E. Trade Center Terrace | Mustang, Oklahoma 73064 USA
1.888.361.9473 | www.tatepublishing.com

Tate Publishing is committed to excellence in the publishing industry. The company reflects the philosophy established by the founders, based on Psalm 68:11,
"The Lord gave the word and great was the company of those who published it."

Book design copyright © 2016 by Tate Publishing, LLC. All rights reserved.
Cover design by Joana Quilantang
Interior design by Mary Jean Archival

Published in the United States of America

ISBN: 978-1-68187-513-2
1. Religion / Christian Life / General
2. Religion / Christian Life / Inspirational
15.11.10

To Diana Craig
for her years of taking me to my medical appointments for Dystonia and then being my spokesperson when I was unable to talk to a doctor or make future appointments.
Also, to Bonnie Hauser and Tanya Zickefoose. Without
your help, this book might never have been printed!

ACKNOWLEDGMENTS

First, I want to acknowledge that this book would not have existed without the Lord in my life.

Next, I want to acknowledge my brother, Les Karns, and his wife, Maria Karns. I love them both and hope they come to recognize the Lord's faithfulness in *their* lives. Without money from them and Dr. Tate, I wouldn't have been able to publish this book.

Finally, I want to thank Michelle Cabaral, Julius Rama, Alison, and all the employees of Tate Publishing who helped to turn my manuscript into a book. Also, I want to thank Bonnie Houser (from St. Paul's Retirement Community for proofreading this for me. If it hadn't been for Bonnie's and Tanya' help on the computer/FAX machine, this book might not have been printed.

CONTENTS

Acknowledgments 7
Plans 11
Introduction 13
Dystonia Basics 15
Prediagnosis and Diagnosis 23
Humanity, Doors, and Windows 27
Postdiagnosis 29
Earning My MLS (Master of Library Science) 35
ST/CD 47
Capable, Strong, and Powerful 51
Bowman Center 53
WC 59
Torsion Dystonia 65
Adult-Onset Dystonia-Parkinsonism 69
Coping Techniques 71

Other Forms of Dystonia 81
Gratefulness.. 83
Contact Information.. 129

PLANS

When you feel worthless and out of touch
He has plans for you and loves you—*much!*
How we handle life is up to us.
Will it be badly or lived with joy?

Your self-worth is about Whose you are.
Have you given your all? You His star?
Self-worth doesn't depend on your health or job.
God can help His child—in a heart's throb.

He wants only good to come your way.
It may not seem so, but it is true
That He cares for you, and you, and you.
He gives each a message tried and true
"I love you! I love you! I love you!"

INTRODUCTION

MORE AND MORE, as I find my health declining and my yearning for heaven increasing, I ask myself, "Why am I still here?" I feel that writing this book may partially answer that question. I often think of the verse, "For me to live is Christ and to die is gain" (Phil. 1:21). To me, this verse doesn't talk about *physically* dying but dying to self and *living totally* for Christ! This thought leads me to the second reason I want to write this book. While thinking about my life with Dystonia in comparison to what life is like for many people Dystonia, I feel so *blessed* (most of the time). I want this book to show others with Dystonia that their lives are *not* over because they have Dystonia. I pray you may realize, "If she can do it, so can I." In collecting materials for this book, I have been astonished and humbled at all the good things the Lord has done since my diagnosis of Dystonia. What He has done in my life, He can do in yours. *He's* ready and willing! Are you?

When September was made Dystonia Awareness Month in September 2014, the Dystonia Medical Research Foundation (DMRF) encouraged people with Dystonia to share our stories in order to create awareness of the disorder. By preparing for interviews with Andrea to write a story for *Senior Life* (a newspaper for seniors living in Michiana), and Marti to write one for the *South Bend Tribune* (local newspaper), I was inspired to write this book.

If telling you some of what I've gone through helps you, I'll feel this book, and all I've gone through, is worthwhile. I would appreciate hearing *your* reaction to the contents of this book. My email address is

libbykarns@sbcglobal.net.
God bless you!

DYSTONIA BASICS

Dystonia is a neuromuscular disorder, meaning it is neurological (a brain disorder), involving muscles. There is no cure, and treatment depends on the severity and location of the Dystonia. Movements usually cause pain, twisting of muscles, disability, and sometimes abnormal posture. There are approximately thirteen forms of Dystonia, and Dystonia is included as a major symptom of dozens of other conditions and diseases. Even though there are many forms of Dystonia, and symptoms appear quite different, *all* forms involve twisting, involuntary muscle contractions. Although Dystonia is a chronic disorder, it doesn't usually shorten a person's life span or intelligence. People with Dystonia may find it difficult adapting their activities to a progressing disability and become depressed.

Activities also present problems when there are side effects because of Botoxes and other medications.

Dystonia is classified in three ways:

1. by age of onset
2. by body parts affected
3. by cause

Concerning age of onset, I found the following chart:

Early onset – before thirty years

Late/adult onset – after thirty years Infantile – before two years

Childhood – between two to twelve years

Juvenile – between thirteen to twenty

Adult – after twenty years

I was forty-eight when I was diagnosed with three kinds of Dystonia and sixty-six when two more kinds were diagnosed. Concerning body parts, Dystonia can be *segmental*, affecting an arm, the neck, or both legs.

Life After Dystonia

It can be *Hemidystonia*, which affects one side of the body. *Generalized* or *Torsion Dystonia*, which affects more than one part of the body, is another way to classify Dystonia. Now besides being diagnosed with Torsion Dystonia and Dystonia-Parkinson, cause is divided into *primary* or *secondary*. Primary means there is no other cause. Secondary, which is what we have, may be caused by genetics, a brain injury, or medicine.

Another way to think of Dystonia is to think it is like a *big* umbrella.

*Generalized/Torsion Dystonia is on one side and Focal Dystonia on the other side.

*Indicates forms of Dystonia I have

Types of Focal Dystonia

- Blepharospasm
- Meige's Disease/Oromandibular Dystonia (OMD)
- *Cervical Dystonia
- *Dystonia Parkinsonism
- *Spasmodic Dysphonia
- Axial Dystonia

- *Writer's Cramp

In case you don't understand my *umbrella* analogy, I'll try to explain the two major types in words. They are *Generalized* and *Focal*. Generalized or Torsion Dystonia (what is one type I now have) is where Dystonia affects any part of the body, causing muscles to twist. Movements may be slow (athetosis), rapid (myclonic), or rhythmic (extreme). There are seven types of Focal Dystonia (although I only have three, which I will identify with *).

Body part affected	Proper name of Dystonia
eyes	– Blepharospasm
eyes and face	– Meige's Syndrome
jaw	– Oromandibular Dystonia
*neck	– Cervical Dystonia (CD) or Spasmodic Torticollis (ST)
*vocal cord	– Spasmodic Dysphonia
Trunk	– Axial Dystonia
*arm/hand	– Writer's Cramp

Life After Dystonia

Meige's syndrome is also known as Brueghel's syndrome and is actually a combination of Blepharism and oromandibular Dystonia. Blepharospasm and Spasmodic Torticollis/Cervical Dystonia (ST/CD) are the most common types of Focal Dystonia and Spasmodic Dysphonia/Laryngeal Dystonia (SD/LD) is the rarest type of focal Dystonia.

~~~

Putting slight pressure near the dystonic muscles sometimes lessens symptoms and is called sensory tricks. The preferred treatment for Dystonia is the Botox injection where botulinum toxin is injected. There are many types of Botox, but they all have one purpose: to paralyze the muscle that spasms. There is always a chance of too much toxin being injected, but that has only happened to me twice out of forty-three Botox injections. There are many variables in having a cold when injected, time between injections, and dosage. What works one time may not work the same way the next time—for different people or the same person. For the first couple of hours after an injection,

I'm usually not able to talk at all. Then I can probably talk until the toxin takes effect, usually twenty-four to forty-eight hours later. For the next two weeks, I may not be very soft; I may sound like I have laryngitis. My voice may sound strangled or breathy, and/or it may seem like I have a bad cough and cold. Also, I'm apt to choke on liquids. I have been in the "side effects" stage for as long as one and a half months and six months! My last Botox was June 18. I haven't been able to talk at all, or not much, since then. I'm not sure what is happening, but I know the Lord is always faithful! After two weeks, I can usually talk better until it starts all over a few months after an injection. Treatments often must be continued indefinitely. In many cases, a person with Dystonia benefits with ongoing rehabilitation therapy. Physical therapist can develop exercise and stretching plans to improve flexibility, strength, posture, and range of motion.

They can also see what types of movements to use so as not make Dystonic symptoms worse. Ultrasound, biofeedback, massage, and relaxation training are sometimes helpful. If orthopedic devices are used, a therapist can help with them. Speech/language therapists and language pathologists can help if there's difficulty swallowing or speaking. Occupational therapists can provide strategies for everyday living in various situations.

PREDIAGNOSIS AND DIAGNOSIS

It all began in July 1993 with what seemed to be another sinus infection. I was working at Calvary Temple's (church) day care nursery school. By October, my otolaryngologist (ear-nose-throat doctor/ENT specialist) decided my laryngitis/asthma had hadn't returned to normal. Between October and December 1993, I became increasingly frantic and frustrated because no ENT specialist could find anything physically wrong, yet I couldn't speak like other people. I was under the care of a neurologist since I was eight, and I was forty-six when I began having trouble with Spasmodic Dysphonia/Laryngeal Dystonia, so I was sure the problem was not emotional or mental. However, I was referred to a psychiatrist who didn't find anything abnormal. Finally, in February 1994, I went to a speech therapist at a voc rehab (vocational rehabilitation services) on Wayne Street in South Bend, Indiana. It seemed strange going there as a *patient* because I used to work in group homes for adults with MRDD (mental retardation and developmental disabilities) (Mental Retardation and Developmental Disabilities) as their *caregiver* and took *them* there! After seeing the therapist, she decided *nothing* was wrong, and I'd talk when I wanted to talk! However to be safe, she referred me to Indiana University Hospital in Indianapolis, IN. At that time, I had my driver's license, but I was afraid to drive to Indianapolis. So Mary Jo drove us to a restaurant where Aunt Dee and Uncle Bill met us. Then Uncle Bill drove us to the hospital in Indianapolis.

Mary Jo was a cousin and my co-Power Of Attorney (POA) who lived in South Bend until recently. After we got to Indiana University Hospital in Indianapolis, Indiana, Aunt Dee and Uncle Bill waited in the lobby when I was called in to see Dr. Weisberger. We'd already decided that Mary Jo would go in with me for my appointment to act as my interpreter and to be

Life After Dystonia

able to tell Aunt Dee, Uncle Bill, and the rest of the family what happened. When I saw Dr. Weisberger, he examined me for a tumor in my throat, but there was no tumor. After the laryngoscopy as advised by Dr. Weisenberger, Mary Jo and I saw Melissa (Speech Pathologist) where I had a Videostroboscopy (*moving* x-ray of my vocal cords to see if they pulled together/apart as they should). Before the Videostroboscopy, Mary Jo asked Melissa how Dystonia is treated. Melissa said Spasmodic Dysphonia/Laryngeal Dystonia (the type of Dystonia she thought I had) is treated with Botox injections. She went on to say that after a Botox, I'd be apt to have trouble swallowing and choking for at least two weeks. She suggested my using a straw to aid in swallowing and to tuck my chin to (hopefully) avoid choking. After the Videostroboscopy, Melissa was sure I had Spasmodic Dysphonia/Laryngeal Dystonia but also Cervical Dystonia/Spasmodic Torticollis and Writer's Cramp. Spasmodic Dysphonia/Laryngeal Dystonia and Spasmodic Torticollis/Cervical Dystonia were diagnosed before 2013 although the Spasmodic

Dysphonia/Laryngeal Dystonia is the most severe. Writer's Cramp only occurs when I use my hands such as playing the piano, using a computer, or signing checks. Although I did have severe problems with Spasmodic Torticollis/Cervical Dystonia for a year, my Spasmodic Torticollis/Cervical Dystonia is also mild now.

HUMANITY, DOORS, AND WINDOWS

Many doors come in all shapes, sizes,
Like a person aphorizes,
When God closes a door, or doors
He *always* opens a window.

Some doors revolve, others do not
Go in a circle? Stomach a knot?
When God closes a door, or doors
He *always* opens a window.

Doors: Temporary? Permanent?
People: Discontent? Content?
When God closes a door, or doors

Some doors are big; others are little;
People are big or little;
When God closes a door, or doors
He *always* opens a window.

POSTDIAGNOSIS

AFTER I WAS diagnosed with Dystonia, I continued to live by myself for six years. Because of my voice, I had trouble controlling a classroom after symptoms of Dystonia began but *before* Dystonia was diagnosed (I had Dystonia six to eight months diagnosis). So after diagnosis, the pastors of Calvary Temple (now Hope City Church Southgate campus) created the position of Resource Director of the nursery school/day care for me. This Nursery School/Day Care no longer exists, but it employed me until I could become a client of voc rehab.

When I first came back to work after having been diagnosed with Dystonia, I remember calmly telling Alberta (director of the Nursery School/Day Care), "The literature they gave me at the hospital says only three people out of ten thousand have Spasmodic Dysphonia/Laryngeal Dystonia. It also says the best way for me to help is to donate my brain to science." I remember Alberta's horrified response, "But you have to be *dead* for that!" I responded,

"I know!" After a day or two, I was *devastated*! I was crying as I said to Pastor Edgar, "I have another incurable disease" (the first was epilepsy, of which the Lord has healed me), and he said, "With God, *all* things are possible." I knew Vera June (a cousin) had surgery for Spasmodic Torticollis/Cervical Dystonia, so I wrote to her and discovered several of the family had Dystonia. When I got Vera June's answer, I again cried. This time, I was half-crying, half-talking with Carol, the bookkeeper. She calmed me by quoting the verse from Isaiah 40:31 that says, "They shall mount up with wings like eagles; they shall run and not be weary, they shall walk and not faint!" She had health problems too, and she later told me this was her favorite verse. She even bought me a paperweight with this verse inscribed on it!

Life After Dystonia

Two months after diagnosis, I had my first laryngeal Botox (the preferred treatment for Spasmodic Dysphonia/Laryngeal Dystonia). Until me, *no one* who had a Botox at Indiana University Hospital in Indianapolis, Indiana responded to a Botox like I did to the laryngeal Botox I had there, but I'll tell you about that in the chapter "SD/LD."

In addition to my duties as Resource Director, my schedule was rearranged so I could be at the church by 6:00 a.m. After Pastor John Wilson talked with me, he arranged for me to be done at 2:00 p.m. so I wouldn't get overtired and could still support myself by working full-time. Besides being Resource Director for the Nursery School/Day Care Program, I was responsible for kindergarteners after they were bussed from kindergarten (at various schools) and before their nap time. I used to teach kindergarten at Calvary Temple Church while there was still a school there, so I'd watch the kindergarteners as they'd play in the gym. Pastor John even arranged for me to borrow a microphone (from the therapy department of Memorial Hospital [a hospital in South Bend, IN, where I live]), so I could read to the children. Also, changing my voice—by pretending to sound like different characters—and laughing helped.

Four months after diagnosis of Dystonia, I had the opportunity to go to Odessa, Ukraine, on a mission's trip. I checked with Dr. Brashear (doctor I saw in Indianapolis) to see if it was medically okay for me to go. She said yes but was very surprised I *wanted* to go because I couldn't talk and get tired easily. Since *everyone* on the team had to have interpreters in the Ukraine, and I knew the rest of the missions' team would help me, I didn't see a problem with me not being able to talk. As far as my tiring easily, I still have that problem. I figured I had a choice to keep on with life or give up and just exist. Since I've never been one to give up, I went to Ukraine but stayed in a hotel we nicknamed "Roach Hotel," andI rested sometimes while the others went on camp meetings every night. Going to Ukraine in 1994 was wonderful and life changing for me. I taught how the Ukrainians were beginning a new life freed from Russia, and I was beginning a new life with Dystonia.

Life After Dystonia

I lived at the house on Manor Drive for six years after being diagnosed with Dystonia. I was ready to move. Before I moved, my family didn't want me to move into an apartment.

Previously, my uncle had enclosed our porch and added a patio to my house on Manor Drive. For eleven years, I was self-employed, running my own day care at home. When Mom died, she deeded the house to me, so me not having to go away from work and not having to pay rent or have a mortgage seemed like an ideal setup—except for *physical problems*! Anyway, after I moved to Fairington Apartments, everyone agreed this move was best for *me*!

EARNING MY MLS (MASTER OF LIBRARY SCIENCE)

I had my Bachelor of Arts from Bethel College and Master of Science from IUSB—both in elementary education before I was diagnosed with Dystonia! I'd taught kindergarten, had substituted in kindergarten, sixth grade, and special education and had been self-employed at Storybook Day Care Home for eleven years! I had to stop teaching because of Dystonia. I didn't plan to *ever* return to school! However, when I was diagnosed with Dystonia, Pastor John helped me become a client of vocational rehabilitation services (voc rehab). They funded my going to Michiana Community College to take a medical transcription program, but I had to leave because of a problem with incoordination. I *needed* to do something to earn a living, so I began another master's degree—this time in library science! I was fifty when I started using a computer. At that time, the only *mouse* I knew about was the *rodent*! When I began earning my MLS (Master of Library Science), a *beginner* computer course wasn't offered. Because Marti had me in classes (she taught classes as well as being dean of the SLIS program [School of Library and Information Sciences]), she talked me into taking an *advanced* computer class before I'd had a *beginner* computer class! I still can't write fast enough to take lecture notes, so I *taped* lectures. When the instructor realized I was taping *his* lectures, he had an outraged (fit) and made me feel less than human. This happened *during* class, so all heard. Anyway, Connie (retraining from being a social worker to become a librarian) and other students went to the dean on my behalf. After he publicly apologized, I continued with the class, but I could still tell I have lack of confidence in my using a computer (although I have *very strong determination* to *keep on* too). The church I went to when I graduated had a mother-daughter banquet the night of graduation. So instead of going to my own graduation, I stayed in South Bend and went to the mother-daughter banquet!

Spasmodic Dysphonia/Laryngeal Dystonia affects many small muscles controlling the larynx (voice box). The first signs of Spasmodic Dysphonia/Laryngeal Dystonia usually appear between thirty and fifty years of age. Women are usually affected more than men. Symptoms are often worse when a person with spasmodic Dysphonia/Laryngeal Dystonia is stressed or tired. If a person with Spasmodic Dysphonia/Laryngeal Dystonia laughs or sings, symptoms may seem better. Voice spasms fluctuate in severity and may even disappear for hours or days. Like others who have spasmodic Dysphonia/Laryngeal Dystonia, people who don't have Spasmodic Dysphonia/Laryngeal Dystonia have seemed to assess my abilities based on my voice, and others have made unkind comments. But I've found most people willing to treat me like a *normal person*.

There are two main types of Spasmodic Dysphonia/Laryngeal Dystonia:

- Abductor, where voice sounds breathy or has a whispered quality and the spasms pull the vocal cords apart.
- Adductor, where the voice sounds strangled, choked, strained, or hoarse because the spasms cause the vocal cords to clamp together.

I have a combination of these two types, which I have been told is harder to treat than the usual adductor type of spasmodic dysphonia. The preferred treatment for spasmodic dysphonia/laryngeal Dystonia is a Botox and is injected into my vocal cords.

Spasmodic Dysphonia/Laryngeal Dystonia is best diagnosed by a team of a *speech-language pathologist* (SLP) who evaluates voice quality; an *otolaryngologist* (ear-nose-throat specialist) who examines how the vocal cords move; and a *neurologist* (doctor dealing with brain disorders) who looks for neurological problems.

When I was diagnosed with Spasmodic Dysphonia/Laryngeal Dystonia, I saw these three people at Indiana University Hospital in Indianapolis, Indiana. Melissa was the *Speech-language pathologist*. Dr.

Life After Dystonia

Weisberger was the *Otolaryngologist,* and Dr. Brashear was the *Neurologist.* My diagnosis was made by Dr. Weisberger and Melissa one day in January 1994 and then confirmed by Dr. Brashear two months later. After I saw Dr. Brashear, it was nearly two months before I had my first Botox. I received my first Botox from Dr. Weisberger on April 15, 1994. Dr. Weisberger is no longer there (the doctor that does this now at Indiana University Hospital is Dr. Stacey Halum, MD, ear-nose-throat specialist). When I had my first Botox, I went into a room where interns lined the walls, and I was told to lie down on the table in the middle of the room. I received *no anesthesia* for this Botox. After I was on the table, I was told to put my head back (so Dr. Weisberger could inject my neck) and told not to breathe! Needless to say, this was a *traumatic experience* that I never *repeated*! When I described this Botox experience at Indiana University Hospital and the after effects to Shari who had chemotherapy, she said the experiences and results sounded very similar! For six months after my first Botox, I could barely whisper, and my right side was weakened, so I'd drop whatever

I'd try to hold. At Indiana University Hospital, I was told they'd never had a patient react to a Botox like I did, so they referred me to Dr. Robert Bastian at Loyola University in Chicago, IL. I saw Dr. Bastian at Mulcahy Center at Loyola University in Chicago, IL, for nine and a half years until he resigned to open Bastian Voice Institute in Downers Grove, IL (also a western suburb of Chicago). When he moved, so did I! I kept seeing Dr. Brashear in Indianapolis for years for the Dystonia until she said I'd reach a plateau. She said my local doctor could write prescriptions for my stabilized doses of medicine. She added that she would be happy to see me again if I needed her to though.

Botox that I had from Dr. Robert Bastian have *always* been different from the one I received in Indianapolis, IN, but I still had trouble until the dosage was repeatedly adjusted. Instead of me lying on a table, surrounded by people I didn't know, told not to breathe, and not given *any* anesthesia, I was to sit in a chair similar to a dentist's chair. There is no one in the room at Bastian Voice Institute except Diana Craig and Dr. Bastian. (For years, she drove me to my appointments, and I invited her to the room where I get my injections). Helga who was his nurse until she retired, used to come and *ground* (like in electricity) me before Dr. Bastian injected me with Xylocaine or Lidocaine for the anesthesia. After injecting some anesthesia, Dr. Bastian would wait for me to cough and then finish injecting the anesthesia. After the anesthesia had time to take effect, Dr. Bastian returned to inject toxin into my vocal cords using the EMG procedure Electromyography). EMG is a technique for evaluating and recording the electrical activity produced by muscles. To break this word down, *electro* refers to electrical activity produced by muscles, *myo* to muscles, and *graphy* to a record of. The signals Dr. Bastian got from the Electromyography machine told him where to inject the botulinum toxin within my vocal cords. Since Helga has retired, Dr. Bastian has done it all. The injection is called a bilateral injection. Even though only one needle is used, it is repositioned within my vocal cords, so both vocal cords are injected.

A laryngeal Botox is an extremely delicate procedure, so even though I finally found doctors in

South Bend, Indiana (where I live), who would give Botox, none gave *laryngeal* Botox for years. Finally, Dr. Savita Collins came to South Bend and *does* give laryngeal Botox. I almost changed to Dr. Collins when she first came to South Bend because of having to go to another *state* for laryngeal Botox and Diana having to take off work to take me there. However, I asked myself, "Why switch now when my getting laryngeal Botox is finally going smoothly, and my dosage is set?" I take such a tiny amount of botulinum toxin and injecting the right amount to a certain place within each vocal cord is *so important* and *delicate*! I have had forty-two injections from Dr. Bastian and hesitate to start over with another doctor. Before each injection, I claim the Bible verse that says, "Those who believe in My name [can]…[ingest] anything poisonous and it will not hurt them" (Mark 16:18). Even though I still don't like what happens after a Botox, I can say I have never been afraid of being injected by botulinum toxin by Dr. Bastian.

I have mixed feelings concerning a Botox not because of the injection itself but because of what happens *after* a Botox. I'll describe the cyclical cycle of a Botox and let you decide the reasons for these mixed feelings. Having a Botox is like an unpredictable rollercoaster ride. Each Botox can have different results (even with the same person and the same dose) because of physical conditions like having a cold, being tired, or because of weather changes. For the first two hours after an injection, I have *no voice*. Then for one to three days, my voice may seem like it was before a Botox. After the Botox takes effect, there's a decrease in spasms. Since my Spasmodic Dysphonia/Laryngeal Dystonia is a combination of adductor and abductor types, my voice can range from being weak, strained, or breathy (like I have laryngitis) for at least the next two weeks. Never knowing what will happen and *when* it will happen still bothers me—especially not knowing how to plan. I tend to have more choking and swallowing problems as this time. After two weeks I can (hopefully) talk better until my voice gradually gets worse and the cycle starts all over in three to four months after an injection. If the "side effects" stages last more than two weeks, a person with Spasmodic Dystonia/Laryngeal Dystonia may be sensitive to

Botox, and the amount of toxin should be reduced. I went through reducing the toxin *many times*, but the "stage of side effects" got to where it lasted one to one and a half months. By 2008, injections were only 0.25 unit of toxin in each vocal cord and lasted one and a half months, so I stopped having laryngeal Botox. However in March 2014, I had my regular appointment with Dr. Kompoliti for all my dystonic problems. I told her I was having more trouble with my voice. Her response was, "Taking a break from Botox sometimes helps when restarted." Even though I resisted restarting carbidopa-levodopa (medicine for Dystonia parkinsonism I take), it *did* help (after lowering the dose). So I decided to try laryngeal Botox again too. On April 8, 2014, I restarted Botox with Dr. Bastian, taking same dose as when I stopped (0.25 unit in each vocal cord). They *did* help, but after three Botoxes, Diana informed me that was her last time of taking me to Chicago. Then I stopped. Currently, I feel forced to leave Dr. Bastian. I have now had two Botoxes in South Bend, Indiana. The first one was okay, but after the second one, I couldn't

Life After Dystonia

talk for three months. Dr. Collins and I agree it *may* be best for me not to have more Botoxes, but time will tell what happens!

Now I'd like to list four challenges in living with Spasmodic Dysphonia/Laryngeal Dystonia. My worst challenge every day is bad for *all* that have Spasmodic Dysphonia/Laryngeal Dystonia, and that is *talking on the phone*, being *heard and understood*! This is most difficult because the person's lips can't be seen. This is very frustrating to me! It intimidates me and tends to cause me to feel insecure, hopeless, and helpless! When people hang up the phone, get cross, and say, "I can't understand you!" or think I'm wasting their time, I tend to get angry because I'm trying my best. Another challenge is *saying anything* although it's *better* when the other person can see my lips than when I'm on the phone. Being unable to be heard and understood around *any talking/noise* is another frustrating problem. Explaining Spasmodic Dysphonia/Laryngeal Spasmodic Dysphonia/Laryngeal Dystonia is often difficult since most people don't understand it even if they've heard of Dystonia.

September is Dystonia Awareness Month, so in 2014, I tried to create awareness by appearing on TV and having articles written in two newspapers. Also, I gave a speech, sharing my story with people. I have recently started being a co-leader for a Dystonia support group at Sanctuary at St. Paul's where I live. When people learn I'm able to speak, I've had three reactions.

- *Disinterest* and ignoring
- "You write out what you to say, and someone else can read it because we can't hear or understand you." (I *tell* people to ask me to repeat if they don't understand me. I know it's frustrating for a person to have to continually ask someone else to repeat, but…)
- Backing me all the way and letting me be free to try to speak. (The problem of others not understanding me was solved by making copies of my speech so people could follow what I say.) This is known as the Eden concept, and I heartily agree with it and appreciate this approach.

ST/CD

SPASMODIC TORTICOLLIS (ST), also called *Cervical Dystonia* (CD), affects the head, neck, and spine. It is one of the most common forms of Focal Dystonia. *Spasmodic Torticollis* is found more often in women than men.

Initial symptoms of *Spasmodic Torticollis* are usually mild. Walking or being stressed can make symptoms worse. *Spasmodic Torticollis* is neuro-chemical in nature (due to chemicals in brain that don't work right) and doesn't result in neuro-degenerative changes like in Alzheimer's disease. One of the most obvious symptoms of ST/CD is neck pain. I definitely have had neck pain, but studies show that 75 percent of people with ST/CD have neck pain. There can also be an increase in the size of the affected muscle. This is referred to as *muscle hypertrophy*. Another symptom of ST/CD is *tremor*! When researching tremor-spasmodic torticollis on my iPad, *Wikipedia* dictionary said *everyone* has a tremor! To prove this, take a piece of stiff paper. Place it on the back of your outstretched hand and arm. After a few moments, the edges will begin to shake.

I have read how any surgery can trigger more Cervical Dystonia even if it is seemingly unrelated. Before more Spasmodic Torticollis was diagnosed following my back surgery, for months I couldn't hold my head in an upright position. Instead, my head went down to my neck and over to my left shoulder. I contacted the surgeon's office who performed surgery on my neck and said they weren't related. Another day, I was in the Wellness Center at Sanctuary of St. Paul's and asked Dave (Wellness Director at Sanctuary at St. Paul's) if he could help me. When he felt the tightness of my neck muscles he said, "That's gotta hurt"— and it did! As when I was originally diagnosed with Dystonia, no doctor in South Bend could diagnose a worsening of Cervical Dystonia although I felt I knew—and I did! Finally, after seven months, I found a neurologist in South Bend who diagnosed more ST but *he* said, "You're too complicated for me to *treat*," and he referred me to the Movementand Disease Clinic Disorder's and Parkinson's Disease Clinic that's part of Rush Hospital in Chicago, IL. Two months after I was finally diagnosed with more ST, I was able to see Dr. Kompliti at Rush Hospital's Movement Disorders and Parkinson's Disease Clinic. Diana, who for years has taken a day off her work to take me to get laryngeal Botox treatments for my Spasmodic Dysphonia/Laryngeal Dystonia, graciously agreed to take me to *this* doctor. To me, Diana is a true model of "Jesus with skin on," which is an expression Pastor Bill (a former pastor of where I went to church) used to use. Two months after my first seeing Dr. Kompliti, she gave me a cervical Botox. For months after this, I once again had symptoms of botulinum toxin (the first time was after my first laryngeal Botox in Indianapolis, Indiana), so this was my first and last cervical Botox.

This morning, I was reading the *ST Quarterly* (magazine about Cervical Dystonia/Spasmodic

Torticollis). In it, they ask to, "Submit information to NSTA (National Spasmodic Torticollis Association) that you feel would be of value to others." This caused me to remember back surgery and how I still feel it triggered a worsening of my Spasmodic Torticollis/Cervical Dystonia (ST). Anyway, I thought of how the following verses helped me through this time. I hope they help you too.

> We are pressed on every side by troubles, but not crushed and broken. We are perplexed because we don't know why things happen as they do, but we don't give up and quit. (2 Cor. 4:8, TLB)

> We are pursued (persecuted and hard driven), but not deserted [to stand alone]; we are struck down to the ground, but never struck out *and* destroyed. (2 Cor. 4:9, AMP)

The verses from 2 Corinthians only apply if we are "filled with His mighty, glorious strength [so we] can keep going no matter what happens–always full of the joy of the Lord" (Col. 1:11, Living Bible Version).

CAPABLE, STRONG, AND POWERFUL

Even thought ST is painful
Through Him, you can take it.
Through Him, you are
CAPABLE, STRONG, AND POWERFUL!

There is no trial
You cannot bear because
Through Him, you are
CAPABLE, STRONG, AND POWERFUL!

God is faithful, no matter
What your case may be.
Through Him, you are
CAPABLE, STRONG, AND POWERFUL!

Libby Karns

God will always provide
A way of escape because
Through Him, you are
CAPABLE, STRONG, AND POWERFUL!

You are God's own handiwork
His workmanship.
Through Him, you are
CAPABLE, STRONG, AND POWERFUL!

BOWMAN CENTER

When I saw Dr. Kompoliti in November 2012, she said she wanted me to again try taking carbidopa-levodopa and to think about entering Bowman Center in Chicago as an inpatient. She explained Bowman Center is the rehab department of Rush Hospital. Shortly before Christmas (2012), Georgian (Dr. Kompoliti's nurse) called to schedule me sometime in February 2013 as a patient at Bowman Center. So when I talked to Georgian (Dr. Kompoliti's nurse), I mentioned my falling. I guess since MRI's have shown I've had several strokes, Georgian was alarmed. Two days later, a receptionist at Bowman Center called (on a Friday) and tried to make arrangements for me to enter Bowman Center the following Monday. Since this was just before Christmas, and I don't drive, there was no way I could make arrangements for transportation so soon. I did call Mary Beth, a cousin in Noblesville, Indiana, to see if she or Bill (her brother who also lives in Noblesville, Indiana) could take me though. Finally, it was arranged for Mary Beth to take me to Bowman Center on January 14, 2013. Mary Beth drove to South Bend and stayed overnight at Mary Jo's house (Mary Jo was the cousin in South Bend who went with me when Dystonia was diagnosed). The next morning, Mary Beth and Mary Jo came to St. Paul's and took me to Bowman Center. Everyone was nice at Bowman, but I was left on the acute floor of an unfamiliar hospital in a city I've only visited for medical appointments. I felt abandoned at first. Mary Beth called once or twice. It was *so* wonderful to hear from someone I knew from the outside! I told her about not being able to do anything on my own, and she asked if I felt like a specimen under a microscope. My answer was yes! I was there for two weeks, so I soon made friends with staff and the few patients who were also able to walk (I'm the only one I know who was not from Chicago). The day I arrived, I saw many

Life After Dystonia

strangers, but the first nurse I saw was Mary Kay, and immediately I liked her. Other nurses I saw during these two weeks were Rosa, Ray, Grace, Kathy, Arlene, Karen, and Martha. I liked all the nurses, but since I saw Karen and Kathy most of the days, I specially liked them. I had never had a male nurse before, but Victor was my night nurse most nights, and I was always glad to see him. My schedule changed every day, so there was a dry-erase board in my room. Cailian, Felipe, Gwen, or another aide came in to my room each night and wrote down my schedule for the following day. During the entire two weeks, I was not allowed to go from my bed to the closet, bathroom, or to the general area for eating (if I didn't eat in my room) or watching TV, etc. by myself; and the door to my room opened into this area. The food was very good though. Since I had occupational therapy (OT) with Beth or Emily and Physical Therapy (PT) with Brian, Megan, or Student Physical Therapists, Lauren or Mary Kate, every day—at least once a day—I soon felt at ease. Dr. Young was my attending physician, and he usually saw me once a day (with a group of residents) when I was

Libby Karns

in physical therapy. I also saw Dr. Tolman many days. Most evenings, Dr. Shannon and Dr. Paul from the Movement Disorder's and Parkinson's Disease Clinic (where I used to be a patient) would come to see me. Also, some days I had speech therapy with Janellem, and one day, she brought Gail to see me. Another day, I met with a psychologist. I don't remember her name, but we had a couple of nice visits. Another day, I visited with an assistant social worker, etc. Whenever I had Physical Therapy or Occupational Therapy, someone had to come for me. Eventually, Emily (OT) or Brian (PT) knew me well enough to let me use the computer sometimes before I had therapy. When I was dismissed to come back to South Bend, Kathy was the nurse on duty. I liked this because I was able to say good-bye to her when I left.

When I returned to South Bend from Chicago, Willie took many things from my apartment back to storage. (I'd taken a lot from my storage to my room before I left.) When I returned from Chicago, I also needed to make a lot of changes in my room so I could better move around my room, get rid of clutter, and

Life After Dystonia

reorganize my room. I was overwhelmed by all the changes I had to make, but when I had sorted books and bought some shelving to put them on, Willie put these shelves up for me. Another recommendation made from my being at Bowman Rehab Center involved my bathroom. First, Emily (Occupational Therapist, I saw mostly while at Bowman) said I needed rails for my toilet, so she ordered them, but they had to be set up in South Bend when I got back to Sanctuary at St. Paul's (where I live). Again, Willie took care of installing these rails. He also placed some appliqués on the floor of my bathtub so I wouldn't slip. I had home nursing care and therapy (occupational and physical) for two months after I came home. One of the things Sandy (Occupational Therapist) helped me order was a bath chair so I could sit while showering. Willie put this up for me. All of Willie's help through this time was really appreciated and something I'll always remember. This help has proved invaluable!

Another change recommended while I was at Bowman Center was an overhead light for my room. Mike is the Director of Housing at Sanctuary at St.

Libby Karns

Paul's, so he arranged with an electrician to put an overhead light in my room. I use *this* every day too and don't know what I'll do if I ever have to move!

WC

WRITER'S CRAMP IS labeled a focal, task-specific Dystonia. *Focal* refers to symptoms being limited to one to two body parts such as the arm and hand on Writer's Cramp. When a person having Dystonia only engages in one particular type of activity, it is referred to as *task-specific*. Writer's Cramp is also called mogigraphia and scrivener's palsy. After typing "Writer's Cramp" on my IPad, the link "Writer's Cramp Therapy" also stated, "Arm Dystonia and Finger Dystonia are terms used to describe Writer's Cramp." Later, this link stated, "Writer's Cramp begins between thirty to fifty years. It affects both men and women." Medscape stated, "Very rarely is Writer's Cramp the only Dystonia," and, "Writer's Cramp is often connected with Generalized or Segmental Dystonia."

(Generalized Dystonia is the same as Torsion Dystonia and Segmental Dystonia that affects at least two muscle groups such as the neck and upper arm or trunk and leg muscles.) In "Treatment for Writer's Cramp," Medscape said that no one knows the cause or origin of Writer's Cramp, but it is clearly established that it's secondary to a disorder of the Central Nervous System (CNS) so that something is wrong in the sensorimotor parts of the brain. Writer's Cramp is not a primary disorder.

Wikipedia stated very minor exertions like holding a book and turning pages may result in significant cramping and muscle pain. Even crossing one's arms could cause pain. Worsening of handwriting, frequent injuries of one's hand, and an increase in dropping items may be early symptoms of Writer's Cramp. Concerning symptoms, Bates states, "There are contra-observations regarding symptoms and contradictory theories based on these observations." Although there has been much discussion as to the nature of Writer's Cramp, there is still no conclusion. The link "Writer's Cramp Therapy" states common

Life After Dystonia

symptoms of Writer's Cramp included have been the following:

1. Symptoms of Writer's Cramp include excessive gripping of pen or utensil, flexing of the wrist, and elevation of the elbow." This article goes on to say that progression (of Writer's Cramp) sometimes includes elevation of the shoulder. After typing "Writer's Cramp" on my IPad, *Wikipedia* said the primary symptoms (like poor handwriting, pain, and cramps) may be accompanied by secondary effects.I have experienced all three primary symptoms listed here and most of the secondary effects are difficulty concentrating, disturbed sleep patterns, exhaustion, mood swings, and a short temper. Difficulty concentrating (I notice this mostly when using the computer, and there is *any* noise.) or disturbed sleep patterns are currently the most bothersome secondary symptoms. Other secondary symptoms I've experienced that are associated with Writer's

Cramp are exhaustion, mood swings, and a short temper. The only secondary effect I don't relate to concerns digestive problems. *Wikipedia* continued by saying symptoms may progress and then plateau for years, or they may stop progressing entirely. If adaptive lifestyle changes aren't made, Writer's Cramp can progress rapidly. I've only observed a gradual progression of my symptoms, but I have made adaptive lifestyle changes such as (usually) not getting overtired and not forcing myself to continue (especially on the computer). *Wikipedia* says symptoms may progress to total disability. I was disturbed to read that Writer's Cramp can be a symptom of Myoclonic Dystonia, Spinocerebellar Ataxia, and Torsion Dystonia. Since my diagnosis of Writer's Cramp in 1994, I've also been diagnosed with ataxia (not being able to prevent going too fast) and Torsion Dystonia. According to W.H. Bates, MD, not only are writers and pianists affected by Writer's Cramp but also telegraphers, violinists, seamstresses, and others who use their hands. Bates says that historically, Writer's Cramp was believed to be the result of excessive fine motor problems complicated by tense muscles, causing bad or illegible handwriting. This is the result of a brain malfunction in the Sensory Motor Cortex of the Basal Ganglia of the Brain.

2. *Wikipedia* Sensory motor cortex or the basal ganglia of the brain. Ross and Paul also mention "embroidery, buttoning clothes, or any action requiring delicate manipulation. *Wikipedia* states that using a fork and knife or shaking hands can be problems as Writer's Cramp progresses. They also added that shaving, drinking tea/coffee, applying makeup, or ironing clothes can cause symptoms to occur (Wikepedia).

Wikipedia mentions EMG as a treatment for Writer's Cramp. Electrical sensors (EMG) inserted into affected muscles show nerve signals being transmitted into muscles even when they are still. Thus EMG can give a definite diagnosis. Muscles tend to fatigue very quickly, and they may respond in different ways in Writer's Cramp. Some may not respond at all, others may over respond, and others may become rigid. I continue to use the computer even though my hand and arms usually hurt because it's so much better than writing.

As in all kinds of Dystonia, Botox is the best treatment for Writer's Cramp. It's often used but is not always helpful. The next best treatment is simply resting one's hand and not using it *at all*! Even writing with the unaffected hand is not advised because of the probability of Writer's Cramp developing in that too. Since I have multiple kinds of Dystonia, I use switching hands or writing with a different pen as the recommended behavioral training. In the article by Bates, not putting any pressure on your hand with Writer's Cramp, such as not sleeping with your hand under your cheek, helps.

TORSION DYSTONIA

Torsion Dystonia is also called Generalized or Idiopathic (of unknown origin) Dystonia. It usually begins around eleven or twelve, so it's also called early onset Torsion Dystonia. Symptoms usually begin in an arm or leg and spread to the rest of the body. I've intermittently experienced difficulty walking, dragging a foot, muscle cramps or contractions, and difficulty grasping objects. In researching Torsion Dystonia, I found all these symptoms. So having been diagnosed with fragments of Torsion Dystonia explains why the above symptoms have sometimes occurred. It is usually genetic inherited from a parent. After my first laryngeal Botox, my voice sounded like my dad's. Even though he refused to be tested or consider anything except his doctor's diagnosis of a stroke, Julie, a cousin who is a retired nurse, thought my voice problem might be from Dad. Torsion Dystonia is the most severe type of Dystonia and usually continues until the person having it is confined to a wheelchair.

A diagnosis of Torsion Dystonia may be missed or delayed. Generalized Dystonia is the same as Torsion Dystonia in the early stages because it may only occur in stressful situations, or symptoms may be subtle.

The first treatment for Torsion Dystonia is usually Physical Therapy. This helps with posture and helps the person gain control over his/her body. The next step in treating Torsion Dystonia is using medications. I've used baclofen and diazepam or Valium (a benzodiazepine), a muscle relaxant. Before I was diagnosed with Torsion Dystonia, I used to take levodopa and carbidopa-levodopa (dopaminergic agents) for other Dystonia Another drug I've been given *before* being diagnosed with Torsion Dystonia is the anticholinergic drug, Artane. Because of side effects such as blurred vision, upset stomach, dizziness, and drowsiness, Dr. Brashear had me stop taking the above medicines. Even though I had unwanted side effects with carbidopa-levodopa, Dr. Kompoliti said that sometimes after stopping a medicine, it can be restarted and helps. Now that Dr. Kompoliti diagnosed Torsion Dystonia, she again prescribed carbidopa-levodopa. At first, the normal starting dosage was too much for me, so it had to be drastically reduced.

ADULT-ONSET DYSTONIA-PARKINSONISM

Adult-onset Dystonia-parkinsonism is a rare condition characterized by Dystonia associated with Parkinsonism due to a neurodegenerative disorder (something in the brain worsens) that progresses quickly. Symptoms I have experienced are foot dragging, Parkinsonism, Dystonia, spasticity (uncontrolled stiffening), slow movements, imbalance, and difficulty speaking. Later symptoms include exaggerated reflexes, cognitive decline, hand tremor, eventual loss of ability to walk, eye movements problems, personality changes, impaired ability to make facial expressions, brain atrophy (atrophy means getting smaller), and increased serum creatine kinase.

Libby Karns

Some cause of Adult-Onset Dystonia-Parkinsonism are coordination and balance problems and neuromuscular conditions such as various types of Dystonia—all of which I have.

COPING TECHNIQUES

General guidelines

I HAVE TO continually remind myself to do everything in moderation. At least once a day, I repeat to myself, "That you will be filled with his mighty, glorious strength so that you can keep going no matter what happens—*always full of the joy of the Lord.*" (Col. 1:11, TLB; italics added).

Another important coping technique is to relax and not get stressed out or overtired. I consciously try to relax when I realize my muscles are tightening. The best way I can do this involves my faith.

I do this by remembering all the Lord has done in my life. Acts 10:34 says, "The Lord is no respecter of persons." What He's done in my life, He wants to do for you too.

Another coping technique I use to remind myself of how blessed I am is quoting scripture to myself such as, "What is impossible with man is possible with God" (Luke 18:27). Another scripture says, "[The Lord] will not in any way you nor give you up nor leave you without support. [he says I will never let you down (relax My hold on you)]!" (Heb. 13:5). Philippians 4:13 (AMP) says, "I have strength for all things in Christ Who empowers me. I am ready for anything and equal to anything through Him Who infuses inner strength into me; I am self-sufficient in Christ's sufficiency."

If I need to refocus on Jesus, I'll sing choruses like, "Turn your eyes upon Jesus. Look full in His wonderful face, and the things of earth will grow strangely dim in the light of His glory and grace." (Helen Lemmel, "Turn Your Eyes upon Jesus") or, "Count you blessings, name them one by one. Count your blessings, see what God has done. Count your blessings, name them one by one, and it will surprise you what the Lord has

Life After Dystonia

done" (Johnson Oatman, Jr., "Count Your Blessings"). I'll also use this technique with other lyrics such as, "Why worry when you can pray? Trust Jesus, He'll be your stay. Don't be a doubting Thomas, rest fully on His promise. Why worry, worry, worry, worry when you can pray?" ("Why Worry When You Can Pray?").

Getting involved in church activities and fellowshipping with other believers is another coping technique. This technique also relates to Participating in activities at Sanctuary at St. Paul's where I live.

Another technique I try to apply all the time is to help others by being empathetic and "putting myself in their shoes" and always wearing a smile.

Wearing something to remind me to be positive is another coping technique I use. I often wear tops with scripture on them such as, "This is the day that the Lord has made! We will rejoice and be glad in it" (Psalm 118:24), or "For I know the thoughts and plans I have for you, says the Lord, thoughts and plans for welfare and peace and not for evil, to give you hope in your final outcome" (Jer. 29:11, AMP). Also, I sometimes wear a necklace with the serenity prayer/

prayer of St. Francis to remind me that although I can do all things through Christ, not all things are expedient (prudent/best) for me to do. This prayer says, "God grant me the serenity to accept the things I cannot change, the courage to change the things I can, and then wisdom to know the difference."

Since all Dystonia involves twisting/cramping muscles, I've included exercised bands and hot/cold wraps here. I often wear exercise bands at night, and I keep them by my bed. If my muscles continue to cramp while wearing the bands, I pray. And if they still continue, I get up and change activities.

Guidelines for specific situations

Botox is the preferred treatment for all forms of Dystonia. "Writer's Cramp Therapy" says two-thirds of all people with Dystonia use it. Presently, the only Botox I use is laryngeal Botox for my Spasmodic Dysphonia/Laryngeal Dystonia. Before each injection, I repeat Mark 16:18 (TLB) which says, "And if they drink anything poisonous, it won't hurt them." Particularly after a Botox, I have used four techniques to cope. First, I tuck my chin before swallowing

Life After Dystonia

(sometimes this prevents choking). I also drink with a straw because this also helps with swallowing problems by letting me stop the flow of liquid with my tongue rather than simply drinking from a glass. After a Botox, I try to be extra careful on what I choose to eat because foods that are thicker (like puddings, peanut butter, or some soups) tend to be swallowed harder than soup broth or liquids. Also, I used to buy grapes before a Botox and individually freeze them. After a Botox, I could take one at a time out of the freezer and suck on it.

I'm (hopefully) learning to speak slowly and distinctly. I try to remind myself to breathe deeply (belly breathing), think of a bellows going in and out, and speak in short sentences. I read where a person with Spasmodic Sysphonia/Laryngeal Dystonia should only speak when inhaling, but I have trouble doing this. Another major problem resulting from Spasmodic Dysphonia/Laryngeal Dystonia concerns talking on the phone. Sometimes, I'll spell my name by associating each letter with a familiar word. For example, my last name is Karns, so I'll say, "*K* as in kangaroo, *a* like in apple, *r* like in red, *n* like in Nancy, and *s* like in Sam." I tend to get very frustrated or angry on the phone, so I especially try to stay calm. I know I'm harder to be understood on the phone than I am even face-to-face because the other person can't read my lips.

Now I'd like to mention some ways I've coped with Spamodic Torticollis/Cervical Dystonia. Once a day, I stand against a wall and try to keep my entire body against it for one minute. I've seen *normal* people do this, but poor posture is more of a risk for someone with Spasmodic Torticollis/Cervical Dystonia than for most people. If I'm walking and am tired, so my neck wants to turn left and down, I consciously stand as tall as I can. Brian (a Physical Therapist in Chicago, Illinois) told me to turn my neck away from the way it naturally wants to go and hold it for twenty seconds at least once a day. I used to have trouble looking at Cindy (Director of the choirs at Sanctuary of St. Paul's) from various angles, so Cindy solved this problem by letting me sit where I can look directly at her. Another way I've coped with Spasmodic Torticollis/Cervical Dystonia is to wear a neck collar. In bed, if my neck

Life After Dystonia

starts hurting while lying on one side, I'll lie on the other side. And if it still continues to bother me, I'll lie on my back and then use a neck collar. For about a year, I had constant neck pain and had trouble holding my head upright. The following verses helped me at this time.

> We are pressed on ever side by troubles, but not crushed and broken. We are perplexed because we don't know why things happen as they do, but we don't give up and quit. (2 Cor. 4:8, TLB)

> We are pursued (persecuted and hard driven), but not deserted [to stand alone]; we are struck down to the ground, but never struck out and destroyed. (2 Cor. 4:9, AMP)

The above verses only apply if we are "filled with His mighty, glorious strength [so we] can keep going no matter what happens—*ALWAYS* full of the joy of the Lord" (Colossians 1:11, Living Bible).

Concerning coping with Writer's Cramp, using a computer seems my best way to cope (even though

I've cried when using a computer). I try to remember to stay calm by repeating verses like, "My times are Your hands" (Psalm 30: 15), or "May the peace from Christ *always* be present in my heart and life" (Col. 3:15, AMP; italics added). Since trouble concentrating is a symptom of Writer's Cramp, I have been known to sing the lyrics to myself to, "Let Go And Let God" (Let go and let God have His wonderful way. Let go and let God have His way. Your burdens will vanish, our night turn to day. Let go and let God have His way.). Another song I might sing is, "Got Any Rivers?" (Got any rivers you think are uncrossable? Got any mountains you can't tunnel through? God specializes in things thought impossible and He can do what no other power can do.). When using my iPad, typing "Writer's Cramp" and then clicking on "Writer's Cramp: Symptoms and Treatments," I found the following information: not making behavioral changes hastens developing more symptoms from Writer's Cramp. Thus, the following behavioral changes I've made include loosening my grip when holding a pen, not *hiking* my elbow or shoulder, stretching my

Life After Dystonia

fingers or hand, and strengthening my fingers/grip with a machine. After typing Writer's Cramp" on my iPad, the article "A Good Pen Helps Avoid Writer's Cramp" states a pen with a wider barrel (diameter) and a padded grip is best because it can help prevent repetitive strain injuries. Forceful gripping of the pen and pressing the pen onto the paper, awkward positioning of the pen or paper, contact stress from holding the pen or leaning on the wrist or forearm all risk factors of muscle-skeletal disorders (muscle and bone disorders). I read where dictation can be a way to cope with Writer's Cramp, but since I also have Spasmodic Dysphonia/Laryngeal Dystonia, this isn't feasible for me.

OTHER FORMS OF DYSTONIA

According to *Wikipedia*, *Blepharospasm* is a "condition where there is a sustained, forced involuntary closing of the eyelids." This can be involuntary blinking or spasming.

DMRF (Dystonia Medical Research Foundation) says *Oromandibular Dystonia* (OMD)/*Cranial Dystonia* involves uncontrollable movements of the jaw, lip, and/or tongue.

Dopo-Responsive Dystonia is a "disorder that involves involuntary muscle contractions, tremors, and other uncontrolled movements," says Genetic Home Reference.

According to Right Diagnosis, *Paroxymal Dystonia* is a "sudden onset of episodes of involuntary muscle contractions that cause abnormal twisting and repetitive movements." When I looked up *dyskinesias*, this term is connected to paroxysmal Dystonia.

DMRF says *Rapid-Onset Dystonia* (RDP) is "a hereditary form of Dystonia and is characterized by the abrupt onset of slowness of movement (Parkinsonism) and dystonic symptoms."

Genetics Home Reference says, "*X-linked Dystonia-parkinsonism* has been found only in people of Filipino descent. It affects men more than women."

GRATEFULNESS

THERE HAVE BEEN so many people in my life after Dystonia whom I am grateful and thankful to know and who have been blessings in my life! Since there are so many blessings (even now), if I forget to mention a name or something they have done, please forgive me. It *isn't* intentional! Everyone is a VIP (Very Important Person)! As I worked on this chapter, I decided I could write a *book* on just gratefulness after I was diagnosed with Dystonia!

To begin, I would like to express gratefulness for the love, care, and support I've received from Les and Maria (brother and sister) and cousins, Bill and Sherry, Bob and Melody, and Mary Beth. Until shortly before Christmas 2014, Mary Jo was the matriarch of the family who was "like glue that held the family together." When I couldn't live in my house because of a malfunctioning humidifier, she and Andy (husband) and son, Rick, let me live with them for one to two months. While I was living with them, I had cataract surgery, and Mary Jo put drops in my eyes. When I was an inpatient at Bowman Center (rehab at Rush Hospital in Chicago, Illinois), Mary Beth and Mary Jo took me to Bowman, and Mary Beth again took off work to bring me home from Bowman two weeks later. Mary Jo was also my Power-of-Attorney for years. Shortly before her death, she became co-Power-of-Attorney with Vicki (one of her daughters). Vicki and/or Mary Jo took me to get sleep studies when I didn't have other means of transportation. Vicki took me to the funeral home for Mary Jo's viewing. I felt honored to stay the entire time like Mary Jo did when Mom died. Even though *many* people came, I didn't know most of them besides family. However, I did know Socorro (resident at Fairington Apartments) and Delores and Phyllis (friend from Hope City Church Southgate branch). On the day of the funeral, Vicki took me to the funeral home. And then Kim

(David's wife) let me ride with her, Matthew, Abby, and Nicole to the church so Vicki could ride with her brothers and sister, and yet I would have a ride. Mary Beth, Sherry, and Bill came for the funeral, so I rode with them from the church to the cemetery and then to the funeral dinner, and back to Sanctuary at St. Paul's. Mary Jo and Andy had six children, so I'm privileged to have those cousins too—Cindy, who lives in Kentucky; Vicki and Andy, who live in South Bend; David who lives in Minnesota; Tony who lives in Granger, Indiana; and Rick who lives in Culver, Indiana. Cindy and Bob have two sons, Joe and Rob. While at the funeral home, I got to see Joe and Sonja and their three children, Charlie, Andrew, and Bailey. I also got to see Rob's children, Lauran, Larry, Makenzie, and Jaxon, and Bob's mother, Elsie. Vicki has three daughters—Amy, Wendy, and Brandy. Amy and Steve have Briauna, Kiara, Jaylin, Max, and Braxton. Wendy is another of Vicki's daughters. Nathan, Blake, Cami (Cameron), and Abby are Wendy and Andy's children. Brandy is Vicki's third daughter. Her and Terrance's children are TJ (Junior), Tatiana (Tati), and Taylyn.

Brandy used to work in the laundry at Sanctuary at St. Paul's, so for a while we saw each other more than just at family parties. One time, I wasn't in my room, so she left a nice note in my laundry (which I still have). For my last birthday, Tatiana helped Mary Jo decorate, and they had a surprise birthday for me. Andy is one of Mary Jo's son, and he and Carol (his girlfriend) have been such blessings through the years. David is another son of Mary Jo. He and Kim live with their girls, Abby and Nicole, in Minnesota. Also, they have a son, Matthew, who lives in South Dakota. Tony and Dorothy have a son, Weston, and live in Granger, and then other children living elsewhere. Rick and Sheryl have three children—Adam, Anna, and Ryan. Some of the children in the family I've never had a chance to meet, but they are still blessings. Their parents and grandparents send me updated pictures. Bill and Sherry's children are Peaches, John, Joey, and Jackie, but I haven't seen these adult children (or their children) since I've had Dystonia. However, I *have* seen Kristen and Heather and their children. When Mary Beth gave me an iPad, it was Kristen who found

Life After Dystonia

this for her, and it has been such a blessing. Kristen also gave me a fanny pack, which I use every summer. Kristen has two children, Channing and Desiree, and Heather and Jason have Liam and four other children. Bob and Melody have three children—Cecily, Nathan, and Mary Grace. Cecily and Darrick have Contessa (Tessa), Victor, and Moses.

Nathan and Kimberly's children are Lucy, Rex, and Jack. Laurel, Leah Grace, and Eliza Delight are Mary Grace's and Travis' children. Les and Maria, Mary Beth, and I don't have children of our own, but there are many children in the family whom we love. Even though Les and Maria don't have children, Maria's mother (also called Maria) came to Indiana with them for Aunt Dee and Uncle Bill's fiftieth wedding anniversary. Also, one time when I visited Les and Maria, we went to San Antonio and spent New Year's Eve and New Year's Day with her side of the family. It was a blessing to meet them I and experienced the custom of having grapes at midnight on New Year. All four grandparents and Mom died before I had Dystonia, so I haven't said anything about them here, but they were each blessings in so many ways. Aunt Dee, Uncle Bill, Dad, and Royaleen died after my life with Dystonia began, and they were blessings too.

Now, I'd like to write some of what I'm grateful for regarding the people on my dad's side of the family who are currently in my life after Dystonia. I saw my three stepsisters, Leah Carole, Linda, and Suzanne when I was in Texas for Dad's funeral. I also have a stepbrother, Royal, but I haven't seen him since I've had Dystonia. Leah Carole is married to Bill, a funeral director and lived close to the home where Dad died. So they took care of all the funeral arrangements while Les was the executor. Ruth, Dad's sister, and her husband, Ed, live in a retirement complex in Leo, Indiana (near Fort Wayne, Indiana). They have three children, Marilynn, Julie, and David. Marilynn and Earl have two adult daughters, Gwen and Emily. This part of the family lived in Iceland, Bahrain, and Germany and visited throughout Europe, Poland, Egypt, etc. Earl sent postcards to me from various places, and he and Marilynn lived in England. I still have a sock cap and mitten they sent from London, England.

Life After Dystonia

Finally, they built a home in Fort Wayne, Indiana, to be near family. A year ago September, Marilynn, Earl, Aunt Ruth, and Uncle Ed came to Sanctuary at St. Paul's visit and hear a speech I gave about Dystonia. I appreciated this, and we had a lovely visit. We keep in touch with my snail mail/e-mail, but it was nice to see them too! Through Aunt Ruth, Marilynn, and Earl, I keep track of this part of the family. Gwen now lives in an apartment in Arlington, Virginia, and Emily lives in Oregon. Julie is Aunt Ruth and Uncle Ed's middle child. I stayed at Julie and Don's (husband) house near Fort Wayne when I went to Aunt Ruth and Uncle Ed's sixty-fifth anniversary party (I lived at Fairington). Julie has driven Aunt Ruth and Uncle Ed to South Bend to visit twice, and we occasionally correspond and exchange gifts. Julie and Don have two girls, Regina and Rebecca. Regina and Jason had one-year-old Madelyn (Now she's fourteen) at the sixty-fifth anniversary party, but now they have another daughter too, Regan. Rebecca and Paul were fiancées when I saw them at the sixty-fifth Anniversary Party, but now they have three children, Breanna, Ashley, and Joshua. Aunt Ruth and Uncle Ed also have a son, David. He and Ann live in Garland, Texas and have two adult children. I met William and Katie at Aunt Ruth and Uncle Ed's sixty-fifth Anniversary Party as children, but now they are both adults and working. Last spring, Katie graduated from college, and Ann sent me an updated picture (taken at this time) when she and I exchanged Christmas cards. I am grateful to have this because now I can recognize the adults too. I am grateful I'm related to so many people and to get annual pictures of the children where I can see how they've changed from year to year. When Dad died, his funeral was in Nacogdoches, Texas. Since Ann and David live in Texas, Aunt Ruth, Uncle Ed, Ann, and David might stop by and visit me at Sanctuary at St. Paul's when they visit family in Fort Wayne, Indiana, and I hope they do.

Another group that is especially important to me consists of those people attending Radiant Church. The church is shepherded by John and Ramona Wilson. John was a co-leader with Bill Howell on my first mission trip. This trip to Odessa, Ukraine

Life After Dystonia

took place six months after my diagnosis of Dystonia. Caleb (John and Ramona' son) also went on this mission trip before he and Carolina married. If it weren't for John, I might not have been allowed to leave the Ukraine with the rest of the team because I accidentally packed my passport before we got to the airport, and I couldn't explain to customs what was wrong! At the time, John and I were both working at Calvary Temple Church and he proved invaluable helping me adjust to "my new life." He counseled me, made arrangements for my work schedule to fit in with my physical challenges and yet allowed me to work full-time. He also made arrangements for me to borrow a microphone from Memorial Hospital's therapy department, so I could communicate and continue to be useful. Finally, he contacted voc rehab, so I could eventually retrain. While I was waiting to become a client of voc rehab, he was one of the pastors that created the position of Resource Director for the Day Care/Nursery School at Calvary Temple, so I could continue at Calvary Temple until voc rehab accepted me as a client. Also, John and

Milena (granddaughter) came to hear the Bell Choir at Sanctuary at St. Paul's.

Ramona has been very influential in my life too. Ramona was director of the Worship and Praise Team at Calvary Temple, and I was Music Librarian for twelve years. So we saw a lot each other. I had two cataract surgeries, and Ramona drove me to one, and Joan (another member of Calvary Temple who now goes to Radiant Church) drove me to the other surgery. Ramona suggested me using an ipad to express my thoughts when I couldn't talk this summer, and this way of communicating is still such a blessing!

John and Ramona led the group when I took my second mission trip—this time to England. John, Ramona, and I were also in a small group at Calvary Temple. One Easter, I didn't have anywhere to go, and they invited me to their house for Easter dinner.

Before Carolina and Caleb married, Carolina went to Chicago with me on the train to get a Botox when I was afraid to go by myself. After Caleb and Carolina were married, but before Joaquin and Milena were born Carolina, and Caleb took me in their car to

Life After Dystonia

Chicago. For several years, Caleb, Carolina, Joaquin, and Milena have come to the night performances of Christmas programs we have at Sanctuary at St. Paul's for several years, but now they have moved to Ecuador as missionaries. Also, this family has come to bring flowers and birthday gifts. I will miss them but am glad they're following the Lord's leading and now live in Ecuador.

Since Caleb has moved, Shauna, Ramona, Lynette, and Markus take turns leading worship at Radiant Church while John usually preaches; although Caleb, Ramona, Joan, and Jim S., and Jim N. and Susan have also led by speaking. Jim S. has now been promoted to live in heaven. Sometimes, we break into small groups and discuss the topic preached on that day.

Jim and Susan also went on the mission trip to England—he as choir president and she was the person in charge of making a video. When I started going to Radiant Church, Jim and Susan or daughter, Sara, have mainly provided transportation each week. Elizabeth and Jonathan, newlyweds, gave me a ride one Sunday when all the Nelsons were gone. Jim and

Susan also came to get me for the Christmas party that Radiant Church had at Southfield. For Thanksgiving 2014, Susan invited me to their house for dinner and a nice, relaxing afternoon. In all, there were thirteen of us. Carolyn is also a resident at St. Paul's Retirement Center and had met Carolyn's two granddaughters, Holly and Caitlin. I wouldn't have known them without Carolyn or Elizabeth, but they have both married since I saw them. Caitlin has married Matthew, and Holly and Dave now have a baby, Owen. Every year these two families have a picnic at Potato Creek on Labor Day. This year, Susan invited me. I appreciated being asked, and we all had a lovely time. Sara works at Indiana University South Bend (IUSB), teaching English to foreign students, so she invited Sawsan (from Saudi Arabia) who she met through her work. One Sunday, Sara invited another person, Omar, from Saudi Arabia to Radiant Church, so she lives her faith and doesn't leave work at work. Omar was part of Radiant Church, but a few Sundays ago was his last Sunday for six months, and then he is coming back to Valparaiso, Indiana, and I hope to Radiant Church.

Life After Dystonia

Debbie was part of the prayer team when I went on the mission trip to England. Debbie was the person to text at Radiant Church if we have prayer requests (if we have this capability, which I don't), but now Jim H. does this. Debbie coordinates someone or a couple being responsible to bring food each Sunday. Jeff (husband) was a deacon at Calvary Temple and plays the drums for worship at Radiant Church.

Kara is another person I knew at Southgate (Calvary Temple) who is now at Radiant Church. Kara was co-Power of Attorney for me for awhile, so she helped me in many ways. Various people at Fairington Apartments used to ask if she was my daughter because she took such good care of me. She invited me to sleep at her house for two or three days when my apartment was being painted. When I went to the emergency room at Memorial hospital for a broken finger, I left my apartment in a *mess* and took a taxi to Memorial's emergency room because I expected to return to Fairington shortly. However, blood tests showed I had acute kidney failure. Thus, I was admitted to the hospital and *never* returned to my apartment at Fairington! I want to apologize to all who helped me move because I had no idea I'd not return quickly! After Mary Jo (cousin and co-attorney) (cousin and POA), and I decided I'd live at Inwood Hills after I left the hospital, Pastor John arranged for Kara and De to pack everything at Fairington. Pastor John and Kara picked out an apartment for me at Inwood Hills. Pastor John then moved my furniture, and by the time I was released from the hospital, my apartment at Inwood Hills was livable! Kara and John (Kara's husband), Jocelyn, and Jacob helped me a lot more *after* I moved into Inwood Hills. Kara helped me *a lot* with the computer I used to own. Kara came to my apartment and created labels on the computer, so I could organize various papers. When I needed to sell the computer I had, John (her husband) took it and helped me get another one (which I had to sell shortly after coming to Sanctuary at St. Paul's for lack of room). When I had a knee replacement surgery, Kara came to visit and bought and put tabs in The Message version of the Bible for me. Before leaving Southgate, Kara was leader of a small group I was in for Women's Ministries. I spent three to four Christmases with Kara and her family at her grandmother's house. John (husband) came for me. I enjoyed being with Kara, John (husband), Jocelyn (daughter), Jacob, Kristen (Kara's sister), Clayton (Kristen's husband), and Isaac and Emma children), Diana, Kara's grandmother, and the rest of Kara's family. Jacob and Kara used to come early every Sunday and help set up for services (at present, Radiant Church meets in Meadow's Edge School), but now Jacob has moved to Indianapolis to go to IUPU (Indiana University-Purdue University)]. Kara is a certified chef, helps at Hope Rescue Mission, and is part of the Worship Team during Music Worship. When Kara heard I was writing this book, she volunteered to help with names and their spellings, so she is again helping me. I'm proud of Kara and Jacob, and I am glad we have reconnected. Last March, I saw John at Radiant Church, and I was glad to see him again too. Besides seeing John last March, I've seen him at Radiant Church other times and would be happy if he came regularly with Kara.

Others from Calvary Temple now attend Radiant Church. I've known Christina and Tom for years. Their son, Josh, is in Dietary at St. Paul's Retirement Community. I also knew Lori and Blair at Calvary Temple. Even though I still can't recognize the children if they aren't with one, or both, parents yet, I know Jacob, Morgan, Mikhaela, Elisha, Marriana, and Michael are Fleming's children. I look forward to knowing each of them. Jim Hock was an elder at Calvary Temple, so I was delighted when I came to Radiant Church, and he and his son, David, were there. Tammy was Director of Women's Ministries at Southgate (Calvary Temple). I knew Sharon M. before when she spoke once at Women's Ministries at Southgate (Calvary Temple). One time, when Diana took me to Chicago for a Botox, we went to Hope Rescue Mission, and Sharon led and Ramona taught. Another couple I knew when I came to Radiant Church was Kristan and Damian. Kristan was pregnant with Isaac when she and Damian team taught a class in Spanish. I still have those notes. Kristan also spoke in Women's Ministries once, and Damian worked

Life After Dystonia

in maintenance and sometimes preached (with help from Kristan for some English words). They now have another son, Max. Recently, Kristan and Ruth Ann have begun a program for children eighteen months to three years during the service at Radiant Church. Jane is another person from Calvary Temple who is at Radiant Church. For the time I've known her, she had been a Physical Therapist. Soon after I moved to Sanctuary at St. Paul's, I discovered her cousin Pat is a physical therapist at Sanctuary at St. Paul's. Kathy is another dear friend who is now dealing with her fourth round of ovarian cancer. You can see the glory of the Lord when you look at her. Denise is a person who taught the four-year-old class at Calvary Temple's Nursery School/Day Care when I was originally diagnosed with Dystonia. The other Sunday, I was privileged to meet her daughter, Heidi. Another person I knew at Southgate (Calvary Temple) before I began at Radiant Church is Jenni. I knew Jenni from both of us being part of the Worship and Praise Team at Calvary Temple before she was married. After marriage to Jeff, she and I were in a prayer group at

Libby Karns

a Southgate. I had heard she and Jeff had a daughter, Ada. Anyway, her mother-in-law was at this prayer meeting too. Her father-in-law had been in India and had heart surgery (in India) at this time. Jenni and Jeff now have two darling daughters, Ada and Katie. Another fine couple I knew from Southgate (Calvary Temple) is Joyce and John. They had a daughter, Alecia, who was in a wheelchair. They took such good care of her! Joyce is a cancer survivor, and now she's in charge of the Children's Ministries at Radiant Church and is such a blessing! Recently, John's parents, Adeline and Stan, moved to St. Paul's Retirement Community. I knew Stan and Adeline from Calvary Temple and met their daughter, Mary, when she came to help them relocate. Thus, I was thrilled to meet Mary and grateful that Stan and Adeline now are at St. Paul's Retirement Community! Also, Joyce and Sharon write names so people can call each other by name (to aid in being part of the church family). John was a deacon at Southgate and manager at Kohl's (store). One day, Sanctuary of St. Paul's had free refreshments and hot air balloon rides, and Joyce and John both served. I enjoyed both things and continue to wish this would happen again. Now he works part-time at Notre Dame and is very active at Radiant Church. When I was in the Lighthouse Foundation Group, they not only helped facilitate this group (with John and Ramona) but picked me up and took me home from these meetings. Also, John and Joyce went to Africa for six weeks this this past summer. Pam is another person I know at Radiant Church who used to go to Southgate. Her daughter, Kim, was a nurse aide when I lived at Inwood Hills. When I had a luncheon to determine interest for a Dystonia support group, Pam was one of three of us who attended. She now has two foster children, Devin and Jenna, who comes with her to Radiant Church. Others I knew from Women's Ministries at Southgate are Melinda Shauna's mother), LuAnn and Michael (husband), Pauline and Mike (husband), and their three children (two preschoolers and baby Gabrielle/Ayana). Sara, Joan C., Joan Joan S., Sally, Howard, and Robert are other people from Calvary Temple/Hope City Church Southgate branch I was happy to see at Radiant Church.

Besides all the wonderful people I was reunited with from Hope City Church Southgate branch, my church family at Radiant Church has enlarged to include many people I didn't know before coming to Radiant Church but whom I now love. The first person I met at Radiant Church that I didn't know before I started here is Susie. Susie and Joyce are sisters, and both of them are outgoing, friendly, and loving. Jenn and Ruthann have also greeted people as they enter Radiant Church (which now meets at Meadow's Edge Elementary School). One day, there was a lady with Ruthann that I didn't know, and she introduced Wanda as her sister-in-law and said they married brothers. Ruthann's husband is Duane, but I still didn't know Wanda's husband, Daryl, Shauna plays piano for Worship. Shauna's parents, Melinda and Al, now attend Radiant Church too. The first time I went to the prayer meeting at Radiant Church, I met Lynette and her toddler daughter, Bree. Later, I saw her baby, Annalise. I learned her husband was Markus, and Lynette and Lora are sisters. Lynette's and Lora's parents Dallas and Fern, now come to Radiant Church. Carla is another person

Life After Dystonia

I've grown to love. After several Sundays, I learned she has a Mennonite background and grew up in Elkhart. This was interesting to me because Cindy (used to be director of independent living and of both choirs at Sanctuary of St. Paul's and a great friend) grew up Mennonite. Eldon is head chaplain at Sanctuary of St. Paul's, and he is still a Mennonite. Dystonia tends to occur among the Mennonites, and I have a family that were Mennonites. One Sunday, soon after I started at Radiant Church, I appreciated David P. praying with me. Other people I've come to know and love that didn't go to Southgate include Shauna, Darion, Kiernan, McKayla, Rachel, Hubie, Joe, Kim, Melinda, Al, David, Gina, Branden, Elizabeth, Jonathan, Riley, Lori, Greg, Vonda, Ray, Camilla, Jayden, Kristen, Bill, Greg, Tara, Miranda, Jenna, Lauren, Nick, Lora, Toni, Pat, Dick, Joanna, Daniel Jr., Andres, Samantha, Lauren (Lola), and Lauren. Sarah's mom, De, was the person who took me to Indianapolis when Dystonia was diagnosed. I knew Sarah's parents, Don and De, at Calvary Temple, but I didn't know her children, Isabella, Isaac, and Ian. Also, Sara and Dan Archer had a new daughter (Lauren Elizabeth) the day before, and Haley became a "big sister." I met Laura and Chuck and their two girls, Katelyn and Elsie, soon after I began attending Radiant Church. Laura is from England, and I look forward to seeing her every Sunday. At the close of many services, people often divide into groups of four to discuss related questions on the sermon topic. I enjoy this time because I usually find people I haven't met, or at least names I haven't associated with faces. The other day, I was in a group with Tom and Val, and later, I discovered we were in the same Lighthouse Foundation Group together. Before, I was in a group with Carla; Denise was her daughter. But when we met in a small group, I learned her name was Heidi. Recently, I attended a Lighthouse Foundation Group and become acquainted with Terry Beth, Ardie, and Kevin (as well as renewing relationships with Kristan and her boys, Isaac and Max, and Pastors John and Ramona). At one of our foundation group meetings, Tom and Val volunteered to take me to Chicago for Botox injections if I needed to go there. I think I'll get Botox injections in South Bend, Indiana, from now on, but I will always be grateful and thankful to know they were *willing*! Also, when Terry Beth was unable to go to a Compassion for Africa meeting, Tom and Val took me! I now have finished attending my second Lighthouse Group consisting of Joan C., Jim H., Robert, David H. Tammy, Tom, Christina, Kathy, Howard, Sarah, and myself, and myself. I loved both Lighthouse groups I've been in but want to get to know others at Radiant Church, so now I'm in a group with Pam (and Jenna and Devin), Jenn, Joan, Rachel, Susie, Lana, Camilla (and son Jayden), and Miranda. Among other things, I have problems with my eyes, so even though the names of everyone coming to Radiant Church are written on labels so we can call each other by name, I can't always see the labels). I look forward to knowing you/knowing you better, so please tell me who you are if I don't call you by name. Thank you!

Ever since Radiant Church opened, I had thought about changing churches from Hope City Church Southgate branch (Calvary Temple) to Radiant Church. I wanted to go to Radiant Church, but I also hesitated to leave Hope City Church Southgate branch, which was home for so long. Thus I prayed about this for almost two years and had been at Hope City Church Southgate branch for forty-four years when I finally left.

I hardly know where to begin acknowledging those at St. Paul's Retirement Community because there are so many who have helped me live a fruitful, satisfying life after Dystonia. Sanctuary at St. Paul's has now become St. Paul's Retirement Community and is part of St. Joseph's Health System. Jane, Virginia, Flossie, Gus, Pat, Kathy, Tommy, and I now live in the same hall. Rogs use to live here but he has moved to the West Building. Judy, and Ethel used to live in this hall, but they are now in Assisted Living and Greta has moved into her own house. I used to live where Mary does now, and Roger was my neighbor. Because of remodeling, Mina and Ellen have permanently moved to this hall. Other residents in Independent East Campus are John, Delores, Kay, Sam, Margaret, Sue, Esther, Kay V., Donn, Sharon R., Roy, Bill, Rita, and Ann. Even though all at St. Paul's Retirement Community are like one big family, I want to

Life After Dystonia

acknowledge fellow Bell Choir members (Ding-a-lings"). Irene, Roma, Winnie, Lenny, John, Jean Anne, Jack, Bob, Bill, Joan, Wanda, Betty, Kay, and Louisa are in Bell Choir only. Many are in the Bell Choir and the Singing/Acting Choir. These people include Fran, Jeanne, Jerry, Jeri, Mary Alice, Carolyn, Madalyn, June, Edwin, Sharon F., Sharon R., Russell, Sue, Bob, and me. Dorothy Kujowski was in both choirs until she went to heaven in October 2014. Also, Cindy used to be director of both choirs, but now we welcome Tanya as Director. Tom (Cindy's husband) used to help with props and will still continue to help when the bells ring away from St. Paul's Retirement Community. Bob with the bell choir and the singing. Except for Bell Choir, Cindy is retired. I still get to see her once a week, and she's still such a blessing! Tom helps her when we ring away from St. Paul's Retirement Community. Bob is still prop man for the singing-acting choir. Helen is a wonderful accompanist for the singing. Those people who are in singing-acting choir only are Carol, Agnes, Greg, Sam, Leta, Laura, Ernie, Dee, Florence, Jane, Ruth Ann, and Mina. I see Marilyn, Pat, Ray, Goldie, Joe, Emily, Kelly, Ellie, Jean, Mary, Mary Ann, Lottie Bell, "Pud," "Tiny," Connie, and Victor, and many other on the Assisted Living floors of St. Paul's Retirement Community. Irene, Will, and I used to eat at the same table for lunch, so even though we're on different floors, I want to mention them. Others residents who have been part of my life at Sanctuary at St. Paul's are Virginia, Les, Bill, Dorothy, Joe, Ray, Bill, Gaye, Enda, Dorothy, Marguerite, Esther, Polly, Klaus, Virgil and Lanette, John and Mona, Sue, Camilla, Marjorie, Maria, Evalyn, Flora Joan, Ellen and Jim, Joanne, Angeline, Fr. Herb, Mary, Mary and Frank, Les and Betty, Del, Adelaide, Winifred, Jean, Doris Hilda, Barbara, Kate, Vince and Barbara, Jim, Adeline and Stan (people I knew from Calvary Temple), Rose and Dori. I was delighted when Dori came to Sanctuary of St. Paul's because she, my grandmother, my mother, and I have been friends since 1968, and Dori and I have the same birthday. Many friends from St. Paul's Retirement Community are now deceased, but I particularly want to acknowledge John, Helen, Leroy, Opal, Jeanette,

Life After Dystonia

Ann, Dr. Eagen, Ellie, Adele, Irene, Paul, Ken, Mary, David, Lillian, Art, Eleanor, and Marguerite for being part of my life after Dystonia was diagnosed. Ellie and I were closest because I was not only her Greeter, but she and Rick, one of my cousins, worked together at Culver Military Academy, and before I published my first book, I lived with her youngest daughter, Patti, with Darwin, Michelle, and Laura.

The staff at St. Paul's Retirement Center is so wonderful. They know the residents by name and call us by name when they see us. Shari is Executive Director at St. Paul's Retirement Community. She was one of the first I saw when I moved to Sanctuary at St. Paul's. Shari was Acting Director at Inwood Hills when I was a resident there, so I was glad to see a friend even before I became a resident at Sanctuary at St. Paul's. Also, Shari has gone with the bell choir when we went to Grand Rapids and Livonia, Michigan. Wanda and I lived at Fairington Apartments when I[ohange] was glad to see someone else I knew when I walked from Inwood Hills to investigate moving to Sanctuary at St. Paul's. Charmayne and Cindy enrolled me as

Libby Karns

a resident. She also goes with Bell Choir on trips to Michigan as has Mike, Dave, Heidi, Bill, Bobbie, Christine, and Beth.

The computers at St. Paul's Retirement Community and I usually have problems, but I thank Sally, Sheila, Pat, Kirk, Toni, Cindy, Tanya, and Bonnie for helping me.

Sheila and Pat are concierges at St. Paul's Retirement Community and so have very important jobs. Not only are they the people first seen when people from the community come to Sanctuary at St. Paul's, but they sign us residents up to go shopping, to medical appointments, or anywhere on the vans, etc. If we have a package to mail or want stamps, they provided this service. If anyone wants something laminated or paper for a computer, all we have to do is ask, and the need is met. Once I had to have something notarized, and Sheila and Charmayne are notaries. Sheila is also in charge of a monthly newspaper *Trinity* (parent organization) that provides to Sanctuary at St. Paul's. Pat and Sheila do many other things too. Jackie downloaded this manuscript onto the computer and then e-mailed it to me so I could add a note and e-mail it. Even though I had trouble doing even this (and then lost the flash drive it was on), I am grateful for Jackie's help. Two other people I've been grateful for are Eldon and Carole, who are chaplains at St. Paul's Retirement Community. They have "Lunch With The Chaplains" once every other month, and I enjoy this. Also, anytime there is a death, they are there to pray and be there for those remaining and lead the departed one to the hearse. Recently, they showed the movie *Amish Grace*, and I was very moved, and I appreciated this. There are also Protestant services twice a week, Catholic services every day, and interdenominational services on special occasions. Janice was presently the business manager at St. Paul's Retirement Community, but Terry held this position until she became supervisor for the Inn (healthcare section) at Sanctuary at St. Paul's. Ron and Amon or Willie (if one of the van drivers isn't working that day) provide valuable services by taking us residents to doctor/medical appointment, banks, stores, beauty parlors, or any needed transportation. They are busy all day from Monday to Friday, sometimes not even having time for lunch. Everyone in the maintenance department is so wonderful and promptly fulfilling needs! I am so thankful for Anthony, Phil, Paul, Randy, Rick, Jimmie, Willie, Maynard, and Sergio. Dietary is another department at St. Paul's Retirement Community. Heidi used to be at Sanctuary at St. Paul's but has now been promoted. Now St. Paul's Retirement Community is only one of the Trinity facilities she supervises, but she still goes with the bell choir on trips, and it's always nice to see her. MJ (Michael Jackson) was head of dietary, but now Paul is head of the various parts of the Dietary Department. Tracey did supervise dietary in the East building is supervisor in the East Building. Olive used to work in the Bistro, but now she is in scheduling. Billie was usually in the Bistro, but I'm not sure what is happening now. We the residents in the East Building eat in the Vineyard since it was remodeled, and Ron, Patty, Helen (who retired before remodeling was completed) Billie, Joann, Crystal, Jill, Tracy, Lakeisha, Kaysi, Ashley, Taria, and Connie took turns with working in the Independent East dining room and the temporary dining room for Assisted Living. Cindy worked in Assisted Living, and Helen worked there every day for dinner. Now we are eating in the remodeled Vineyard. I am grateful that the hours for breakfast are slightly later than they used to be, but I still don't usually eat in the Vineyard. We can come any time from 11:00 a.m. to 6:00 p.m. for lunch/dinner. At first Brittany, Patty, Joann, Kaysi, Ron, Christal, and Kenijah worked with Beth and Ashley. Only Beth and Ashley are here from before. Michael and another man work as cooks in the Vineyard. New servers are Alice, Alisha, Ally, Deja, Mikaela, Molli, Sharise, Chi, and Dareanna (Dee). We had a wonderful and so helpful Community Living staff in Toni, Ann, Cindy, and Karen! Now, Dusty is in the Inn, Ann has moved to another facility, Cindy has retired, but Karen is gone. Bonnie is now Director of Assisted Living and Tanya is Director of Independent Living and the Singing/Acting Choir and assists in Bell Choir. There have been many changes, but Bonnie and Tanya are wonderful! Monica still volunteers, and she is a wonderful help. We have many of the same interests—writing poetry and books and history, so I'm delighted she's here. Amy comes to Sanctuary at St. Paul's regularly to provide services of a seamstress besides her regular commitments as a pastor's wife. Lawrence teaches Tai Chi and Chi Gong and performs acupuncture. Yoga, Pilates, Senior Fit, Line Dancing, Floral Design, Haiku Poetry Group, Traditional Rug Hooking, Woodworking, and Watercolor classes, plus Reflexology and Reike are also offered. An annual arts and crafts fair and a modeling show (coordinated with a local store like Chico's) are also found at St. Paul's Retirement Community. Concerning support groups, St. Paul's Retirement Community has an Alzheimer's, dementia, and "Guys and Dolls" bereavement support group, and a support group named "Living with "Living With Dystonia." I want to thank Amber, Lawrence, Dave, Charlene, and all who have spoken at these meetings. Also, I want to thank Carolyn Pauline, Esther, Flossie, Suzy, Branden, Catherine, Grace, Frank, and all who have attended these meetings. St. Paul's Retirement Community also

Life After Dystonia

provides access to various restaurants, plays, musical, symphonies, and concerts in the community. Until recently, St. Paul's Retirement Community had two stores and two libraries, but this is now reduced because of staffing. Pam used to bring books from Mishawaka-Penn-Harris Public Library, but now Karen come to St. Paul's Retirement Community once a month from Mishawaka-Penn-Harris Library to exchange books. Another perk is that we residents have beauticians (Sue, Kathy, and Jennifer), and they all help each of us look pretty. Currently, Michelle from Teacher's Credit Union and podiatrists, Dr. Moore (Deb and Carla are her assistants) and Dr. Worden, come to St. Paul's Retirement Community. Amber is head of the Therapy Department at St. Paul's Retirement Community, and is in charge of excellent therapists. Lisa, Pyel, Kari, and Pat still work in the therapy department, but I haven't seen Katie or Stacie. Also, there are some new people, but I don't know there names. I think I've had each one at some time and want to express how grateful and thankful I am for each one of them. Jackie was Director of Nursing for Assisted Living but now Tamara is Director of Nursing for Assisted Living. Tamara has her office on the floor where Independent Living residents live. Mike is Director of Housing for all of St. Paul's Retirement Community, but his office is now where the East Independent Living residents live. Last spring, St. Paul's Retirement Community offered services for a (Nurse Practitioner). Jamie was the first nurse practitioner, and when she moved, Elizabeth became the new Nurse Practitioner, and now Luda is another Nurse Practitioner. Luda only works part-time, so Shari (Director of St. Paul's Retirement Community) is looking for a full-time Nurse Practitioner. Since this service has been provided, Linda has done an excellent job as secretary and Medical Assistant. She has also helped me get my medical records from Rush Hospital and other times I've needed help on the phone. When Luda ordered blood tests, Shelby (phlebotomist) comes to my room, and she always draws blood the first time (I've been stuck as many as ten times for one blood draw). Tony has been social worker in the West Building, but now

Life After Dystonia

Max is social worker for the East Building. Many residents have helpers like Dale, Kay, Marlene, Tina, and Marcy who offer help through various organizations. Even though I've never used the services of such organizations, I see people from them and enjoy seeing and visiting with them. Also, St. Paul's Retirement Community has wonderful aides like Martha, Lakeisha, and nurses like Raechel, and Richard. Toni C. was supervisor of housekeeping, but Deb is now supervisor of laundry at St. Paul's Retirement Community. Debbie S. cleans the rooms on the floor where I live. If she's unavailable, Deb, Sandy, Lorna, or Rose or someone from another part of St. Paul's Retirement Community helps on this floor. Dave is (Capitals_wellness director at St. Paul's Retirement Community and his office is in the (Capitals) wellness room. Ashley interned with him, but is no longer at St. Paul's Retirement Community.

There are so many people at Calvary Temple/Hope City Church Southgate branch for who I am thankful! I will begin with Alberta. She has been such a blessing *so many times* and still is such a blessing!

Libby Karns

She was Director of the Day Care-Nursery Nursery school of Calvary Temple when my Dystonia was diagnosed. And then she was Music Secretary while I was Music Librarian, and now she is Business Manager for Calvary Temple/Hope City Church Southgate branch. I have been grateful to know Chris (husband) too. I watched her children, John and Amy, grow up. John married Melissa who was a church secretary at Calvary Temple. Together, they pastured a church and had their first child, Hannah. Just since I left this church, Amy has married too. Bob and Arlene (Chris's parents) were also active at Calvary Temple/Hope City Church Southgate branch. He was an elder, and I remember peacefully picketing with Arlene, carrying signs concerning "Right to Life." Also, their daughter Martha, and I were in a small group in Woman's Ministries at Calvary Temple/Hope City Church Southgate branch. Another family I would like to mention is the Howells. I have known Pastor Bill and Linda before they were married, and now they are grandparents. Brother Bill and Lois were Linda's parents, and Bill and June and Bill were

Life After Dystonia

Pastor Bill's parents. Pastor Bill and Linda were both team members of the worship and praise team at Calvary Temple/Hope City Church Southgate branch. Pastor Bill and Linda have two boys, Joshua and Nathan. Pastor Bill and Pastor John led a team from Calvary Temple/Hope City Church Southgate branch to Ukraine, and Linda and Joshua were part of this team. Pastors Bill, John, and Edgar created the position of Resource Director of the Nursery School Day Care at Calvary Temple after I was diagnosed with Dystonia, allowing me to continue to be self-sufficient in *Christ's* sufficiency. Pastor Edgar became head pastor at Calvary Temple/Hope City Church Southgate branch when Pastor Bill left to become Vice President of Next Level International (NLI), a mission's organization. I never knew Pastor Edgar's dad, but his mom, Mary, and I were secret pals for one year and have remained sisters in the Lord. When Pastor Edgar married Cynthia, he became the son-in-law of Jackie and John who are active members of Calvary Temple/Hope City Church Southgate branch. Pastor Edgar and Cynthia have four sons, Brandon,

Austin, Maxwell, and Garett. All of them but Garett are married, and Austin and his wife have recently had a baby. Two or three days after I was diagnosed with Dystonia, I saw Pastor Edgar. I was crying and saying, "This is the second incurable disease I've been diagnosed with." I'll never forget how I felt when he said, "*Nothing* is incurable with God." Pastor Edgar has an older brother, Noe, who was a past president of the choir and married Tracy. Pastor Edgar also has another brother, Eddie. Cynthia also has brothers and sisters, but the only one attending Calvary Temple/Hope City Church-Southgate Branch now is Joanna and her girls. The most recent pastor I had at Calvary Temple/Hope City Church Southgate branch was Pastor Steve. I want to thank him and his family for his filling in as interim pastor and for his wonderful messages.

I told Pastor Bill, Linda, and Joshua about being part of the team for my first mission trip, but Pastor John coled this trip, and other team members were Caleb, Stan, Phil, Melissa, Dale, Jim and Ellen, Risa, and Martha. We also had four interpreters, Nadya, Tanya, Laura, and Lena.

Life After Dystonia

Uri and Stephen were Ukrainian drivers, and Pastor Raphael was the Ukrainian pastor. Matt was the employee from Next Level International, the sponsoring mission's organization. To coin a phrase from Pastor Bill, all the above people were "Jesus with skin on." Even though this trip was wonderful and life-changing, I couldn't have made it without all of them. Besides Pastor Bill, the only other person still at Calvary Temple/Hope City Church Southgate branch is Dale. Before I had Dystonia, I had his sister, Lisa, as a student in kindergarten, and I knew his mother, Delores, from that time. Also, I took care of his three children—Josh, Jason, and Jamie—before school, previous to being diagnosed with Dystonia. Kathy, another sister of his, married Jim. Kathy was part of the bus ministry at Calvary Temple when they provided this service, and Jim printed bulletins and has been an usher for many years. Rex, Sandy, and I were team members when we went to England on a mission trip. They have a daughter, Teri, who is a missionary with Rick (her husband) in Africa. Others on this mission trip I am thankful for are

John, Ramona, Kelly, Kim, Ann, BJ, Donna, Stuart, Debera, Jeanine, Leann, Debbie, Jim N., Susan, Jim K., and Kay. Janet and later the De Craene family (Eric, Carrie, Nathan, and William) provided transportation to Calvary Temple/Hope City Church Southgate branch while Delores faithfully took me to Uplifters (a church group at Calvary Temple/Hope City Church Southgate branch). Janet and I sat together while she was part of Calvary Temple/Hope City Church Southgate branch. She also took me to a class in Spanish. Kristan and Damien's team taught at Calvary Temple/Hope City Church Southgate branch before they moved to Radiant Church. Janet had been taking me to Southgate, but after I broke my foot, Janet quit going to any church. While I was unable to go to Southgate, Carrie came to visit me. Out of these visits, she volunteered for her family to take me to church, so I met Eric and their two boys. Eric, Carrie, Nate, and Will were always so faithful. Sometimes, Carrie's mom came up from Logansport, Indiana, and went to church with us. Eventually, they moved to Arizona so I started going to Radiant Church.

Life After Dystonia

For years, Diana was so supportive and faithful in taking off work to take me to medical appointments in Chicago. Her supervisor and colleagues were also helpful in scheduling/switching with Diana so she would be free to take me. One time, when Diana hurt her foot and couldn't drive, her parents came from Peru and drove Diana and me to Rush Hospital's Movement Disorders and Parkinson's Disease Clinic for my appointments in Chicago, Illinois. Sara (Diana's sister) used to live with Diana before she and Roger got married, so the three of us went many places together. Before Diana and Roger married, Andrea (one of Diana's daughters) got married, and Erica (another daughter) and Diana invited me to a shower they gave for her. One Christmas, I went to Paula (Diana's sister) and Peter's (husband) house. By the Thanksgiving after this, Paula and Peter had a new house, so I went here for Thanksgiving. After Diana and Roger married, I went to their house for Thanksgiving another year. It was here I met Gordy. Sara, Pat and Joe (Diana's Mom and Dad), Paula (Diana's sister) were also there. This Thanksgiving I wore a neck collar because I couldn't hold my head up due to having been given too much botulinum toxin when I had a cervical Botox. Another year, I went to Dave (Diana's brother) and Amber's (wife) house for Christmas. The above adults were there, but Elijah, Owen, and Reuben (Dave and Amber's three boys), Peter (Paula's husband), and their two children, Melody and Isaac, were also there. Also, Erica (Diana's daughter) and Joel (her husband) and their two children, Braden and Audra, were there.

I especially looked forward every Sunday to Sherry's big smile and her asking, "How's Libby Lou?" (Mom's name was Louise, so I like Sherry saying Libby Lou). Sherry, Austin, and some others from Calvary Temple/Hope City Church-Southgate branch brought me flowers on Mother's Day, and one year, they had an outreach and brought flowers for many residents at Calvary Temple. Barbara (Sherry's mom) used to be a church secretary at Calvary Temple, so I'm also thankful to her for many things.

Once before Christmas, I was surprised by carolers led by Jennifer and Carol. Jennifer and Carol led this

Life After Dystonia

group of missionette girls at Calvary Temple/Hope City Church Southgate branch to my room at Sanctuary of St. Paul's. I recognized Chelsea, Allison, and many other girls. I and all my neighbors really appreciated this and thought this was so nice!

I would also like to express gratitude to and for Margaret, Chris, Phyllis, Carolyn, Kenny Terri, Lola, Richard, Donna, Tina, Diana, Al, Jo, Dee, Margie, Norma, Mary, Kim, Dave, Julie Jim, Cheryl, Jan, Mike, Jennifer, Julie, Roger, Marilyn, Tammy, Missy, Debbie, and all the other many wonderful people at Calvary Temple/Hope City Church Southgate branch.

Everyone in the medical field has played a very important role in my life after Dystonia. First, I'd like to mention Dr. Kazmierzak, her nurse, Amber (Michelle was her nurse during my first four years with Dr. Kazmierzak), Lisa and the other receptionists/assistants, and doctors who helped when Dr. Kazmierzak was unavailable at Ireland Road Clinic. I also want to thank Dr. Bastian and his staff when I went to Downer's Grove, Illinois (suburb of Chicago), for laryngeal Botox. I also want to express gratefulness to Dr. Collins for coming to South Bend and enabling me to get laryngeal Botox in South Bend, Indiana.

In 2008, Dr. Mitros performed a total knee replacement.

In 2012, Dr. Kristl diagnosed more Spasmodic Torticollis/Cervical Dystonia after six months of no doctor in South Bend, Indiana, being able to find out what was wrong. Dr. Kristl referred me to Dr. Kompoliti at the Movement Disorders and Parkinson's Disease Clinic (part of Rush hospital in Chicago, Illinois), and I'm grateful to her for so much. Particularly, in retrospect, I'm glad I was able to be an inpatient at Bowman Center (rehab for Rush Hospital in Chicago, Illinois, and the Movement Disorders and Parkinson's Disease Clinic is part of this medical complex). I liked everyone at Bowman, and everyone was helpful. I spent the most time with Mary Kay, Kathy, Karen, Cailon, Victor, Ray, Brian, and Emily, so I especially want to express appreciation to them. I am also impressed with the service from dietary and the social workers, making arrangements with Amedysis for Kathy (physical therapist), Sandy (occupational

Life After Dystonia

therapist), and Dolly (nurse) coming to my room to provide their services. The frame with arms to go over the toilet that Emily ordered and the shower chair that Sandy ordered have been invaluable and are used regularly. Finally, I want to thank Dr. Magnuson and Julie, Krista, Tara, Molly, and Margaret for being friends and providing wonderful dental service. Unlike many people, like going to the dedntist!

I want to express gratitude to Maureen McFadden for airing an interview on Channel 16 TV-News. This was about Dystonia and me in preparation for Dystonia Awareness Month. Also, I want to thank Andrea, Deb (from Senior Life), and Marti (from the South Bend Tribune) for writing my story to help promote this month. From St. Paul's Retirement Community, Jessica and Cindy really helped me when I gave a speech about Dystonia. Also, it was wonderful of Aunt Ruth, Uncle Ed, and cousins Marilynn and Earl to come from Ft. Wayne, Indiana, to hear me. From the above publicity, Frank and I became coleaders of a Dystonia support group at St. Paul's Retirement Community in South Bend, Indiana. Janet and Veronica (President and educational director of DMRF—Dystonia Medical Research Foundation) have been faithful in inviting people with Dystonia to the meeting. Cindy and Monica have helped each month by creating and putting flyers around St. Paul's Retirement Community. Now, Tanya and Monica do this. I want to thank everyone who came to these meetings. Amber, Lawrence, Dave, Frank, Charlene, and Barbara agreed to speak when I didn't have a speaking voice.

CONTACT INFORMATION

BASTIAN VOICE INSTITUTE (I used to see Dr. Robert Bastian for Botox injections for my spasmodic dysphonia)
3010 Highland Parkway, Suite 550
Downer's Grove, IL 60515
PH.: (630) 724-1100
FAX: (630) 724-0084
Web address: www.bastian.voice.com

DR. COLLINS, SAVITA
211 Eddy Street (South Bend Clinic)
Otolaryngology Department
South Bend, IN 46617
PH.: (574) 237-9200

Dystonia MEDICAL RESEARCH FOUNDATION (DMRF)
One East Wacker Drive, Suite 2810
Chicago, IL 60601-1905
Ph: 312 755-0198; or
Toll free at 800-377-3978
FAX: 312 803-0138
Email: Dystonia@Dystonia-foundation.org

MOVEMENT DISORDERS AND PARKINSON'S DISEASE CLINIC
1725 West Harrison Street, Suite 755
Chicago, IL 60612
Ph.: (312) 563-2900
FAX: (312) 563-2024
Email: movement_disorder@rush.edu

SPASMODIC DYSPHONIA/LARYNGEAL Dystonia
300 Park Boulevard
Suite 335
Itasca, IL 60143
Magazine: Our Voice

PH.: (800) 795-6732
FAX: (630) 250-4505
Email: NSDA@dysphonia.org
Website: www.dysphonia.org

SPASMODIC TORTICOLLIS/CERVICAL Dystonia
Magazine: ST Quarterly
Orange County Memorial Medical Center
Fountain Valley, CA 92708
PH.: (714) 378-9837; or Toll-free @ (800) 487-8385
Email: NSTAmail@aol.com
Web address: www.torticollis.org